Text and drawings copyright ©Carla Jennings 2015

The right of Carla Jennings to be identified as the Author of the work has been asserted by her in accordance with the Copyright, Designs and Patents Act 1988.

Published in 2015 by ArtCircus Books
ISBN 978-1-909644-91-5

All rights reserved. No part of this publication may be reproduced, stored in a retrieval system or transmitted in any form, or by any means, without the prior written permission of the publisher, nor be otherwise circulated in any form, binding or cover other than that in which it is published and without a similar condition being imposed on the subsequent purchaser.

Our Patterned World

Carla Jennings

Our Patterned World

I grew up in Cornwall, surrounded by stunning scenery, beautiful countryside, the gorgeous coastline & lots of artistic, creative people.
Since being a young child I've just loved being involved in as many different types of arts & crafts as I can get my hands on. One of my earliest memories is using felt tip pens & filling graph paper with leaf shapes to form geometric patterns. Over the years, I've also enjoyed card making, mosaics, paper collage, mixed media collage & developed a real passion for painting with pastels as a teenager. There tends to be a massive void in my life if I'm not using my hands to create something.

I ran a successful silver jewellery making business for 8 years before giving birth to my beautiful daughter 3 years ago. With a small one now in tow, I felt it was time for a change in career. I was super excited when I stumbled across zentangle, an art form similar in principle to ornamental art, using repetitive patterns to create beautifully intricate images. This ended up being the perfect inspiration for me as I started to combine the idea of these intricate patterns with the experience I'd already gained from my artistic background.

I would love for this book to bring some extra happiness to your life. For me, artwork & colour combinations can often add joy, excitement or even a smidge of comfort to my life. The drawings in this book are for you to enjoy, for you to add your own stamp of creativity & imagination.

This book has developed from a collection of photographs I've taken over the past few months, mainly photos from the gardens & wild hedgerows around where I live in Cornwall. The shapes & patterns within a single flower or leaf, the patterns & textures on the feathers of a simple bird, the intricate shapes within a butterfly's wing & the flowing, organic forms in the creation around us all fascinate & excite me. I really do believe that the best patterns can be found in nature. As you look through each design in this book, you may be able to see where my inspiration has come from; for all you gardeners & nature lovers, keep your eye out for designs inspired by a Camellia flower, apple blossom, primrose, echinacea & aquilegia, candy tuft, alstromeria, rhododendron, tulips, clover, dandelion, allium & you may even be able to spot the astrantia.

I've loved every minute of drawing & designing so far & hope you will cherish this colouring book, that you will put aside some time just for you to relax & get those creative juices flowing.

All the patterns in this book are drawn mainly using UniPin Fine Line pens. I tend to work with a 0.3 nib, a 0.1, 0.05 & for extra fine details I have a Copic Multiliner 0.03 . You will notice throughout the book that the drawings gradually range from simple to more detailed. You may wish to colour the simple drawings as they are or add your own details & patterns to them, using any pen you feel comfortable with. The finer the pen, the more detail you will be able to add. For colouring the more detailed drawings towards the back of the book you may find you need to use a finer pen or brush, or you can ignore the extra details by colouring over them.

For adding beautiful colours in your own style, choose the art materials you feel fits with your personality, or choose the materials you enjoy using the most. Because of the thickness & texture of this paper, I would recommend either using coloured pencils which are fantastic for blending & shading or bright ink pens for a bold illustrative look. Watercolour pencils or paints can add fluidity & a beautiful softness to your pictures, but I would recommend that you place a few sheets of paper underneath your painting to protect the pages underneath.

Experiment & have fun!

Carla

"Blessed are they who see beautiful things in humble places where other people see nothing"
Camille Pissarro

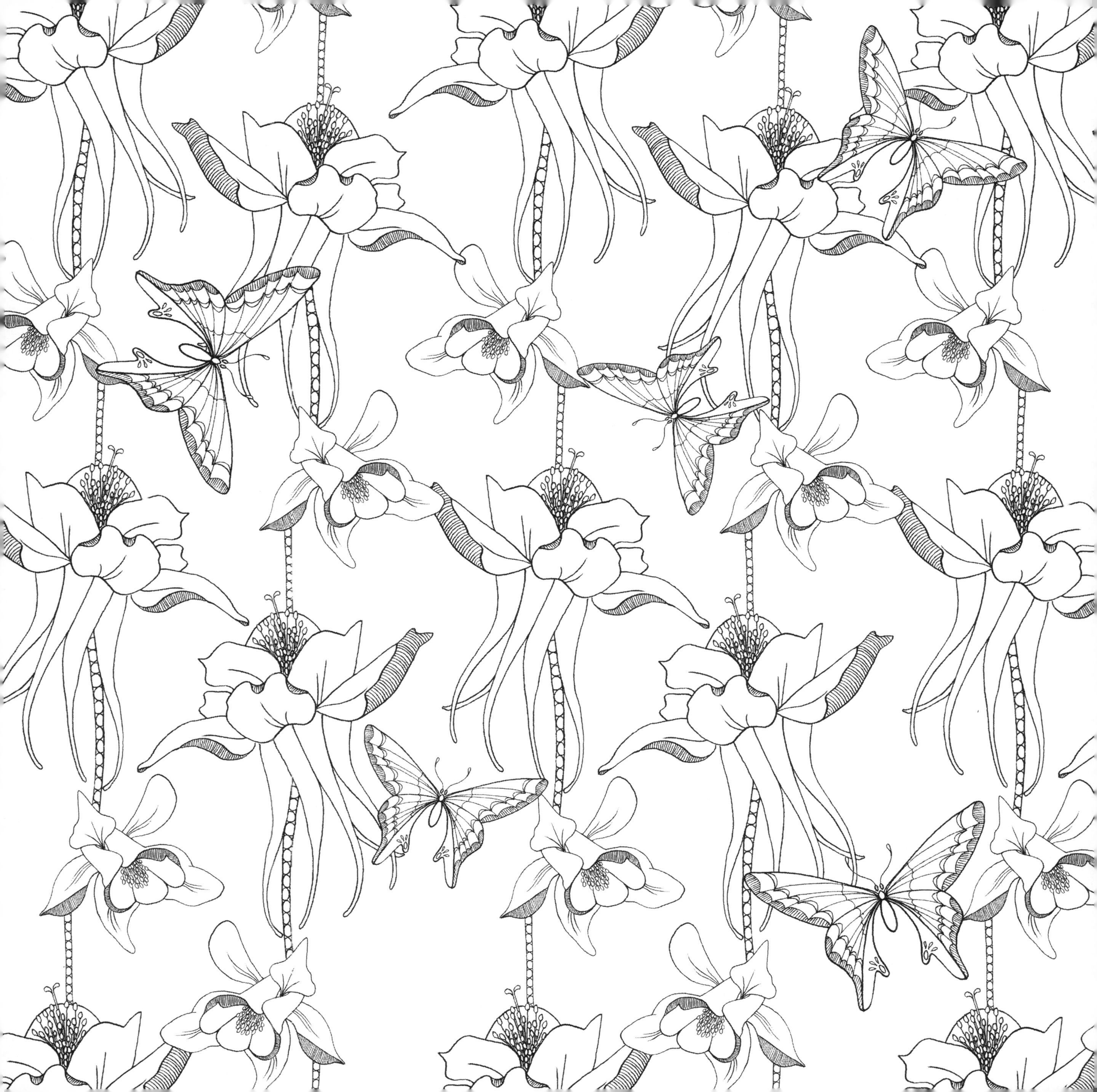

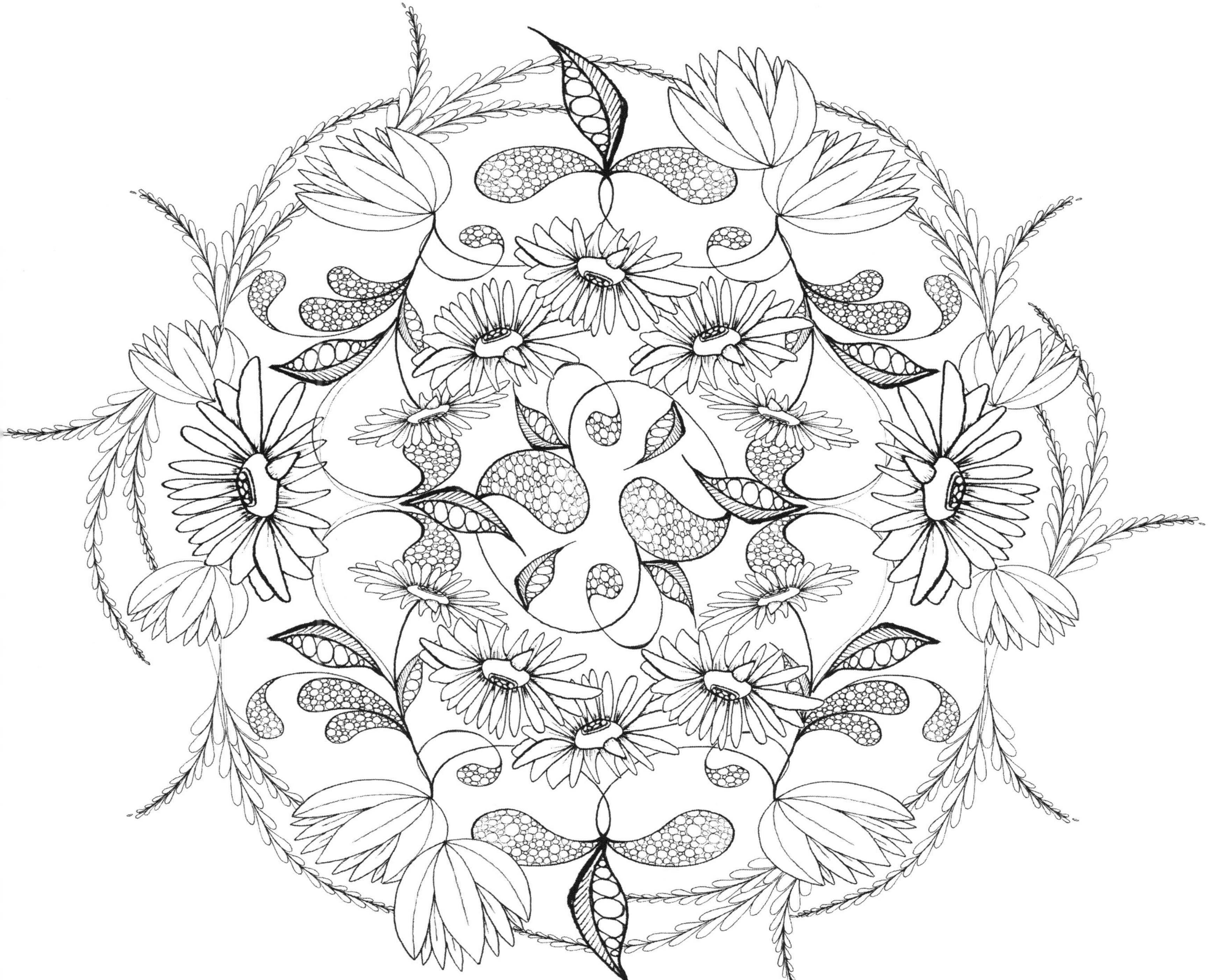

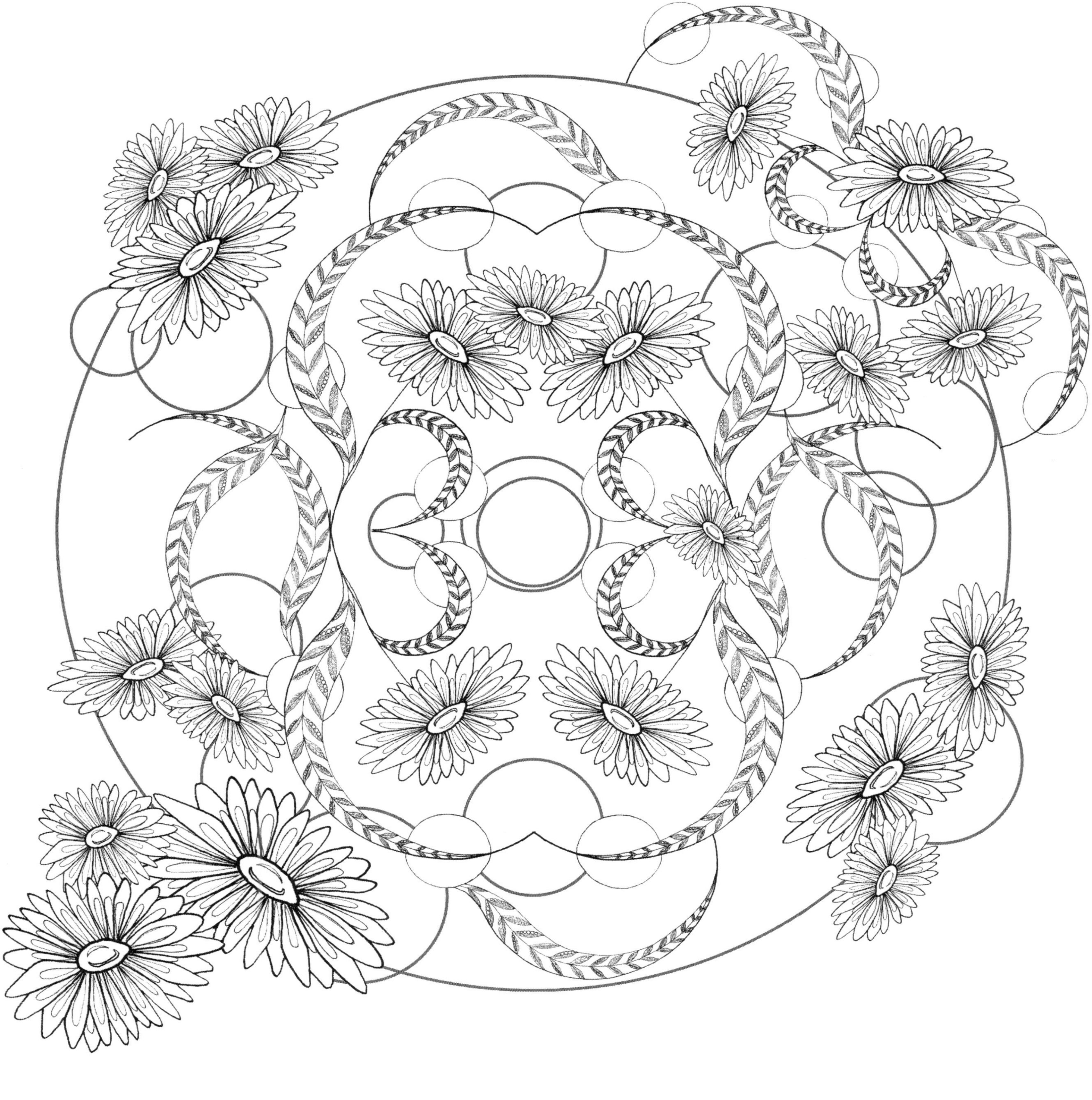

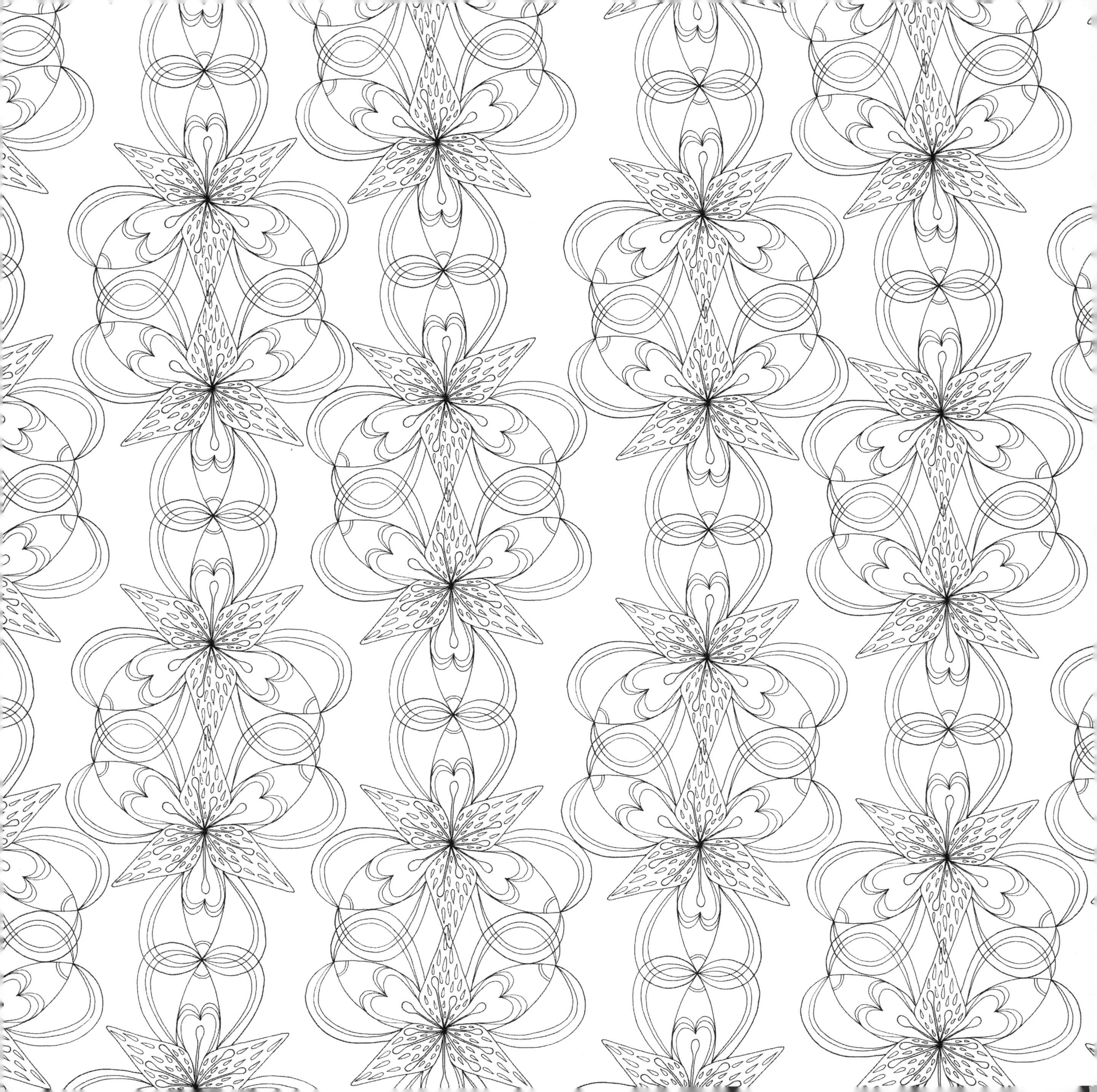

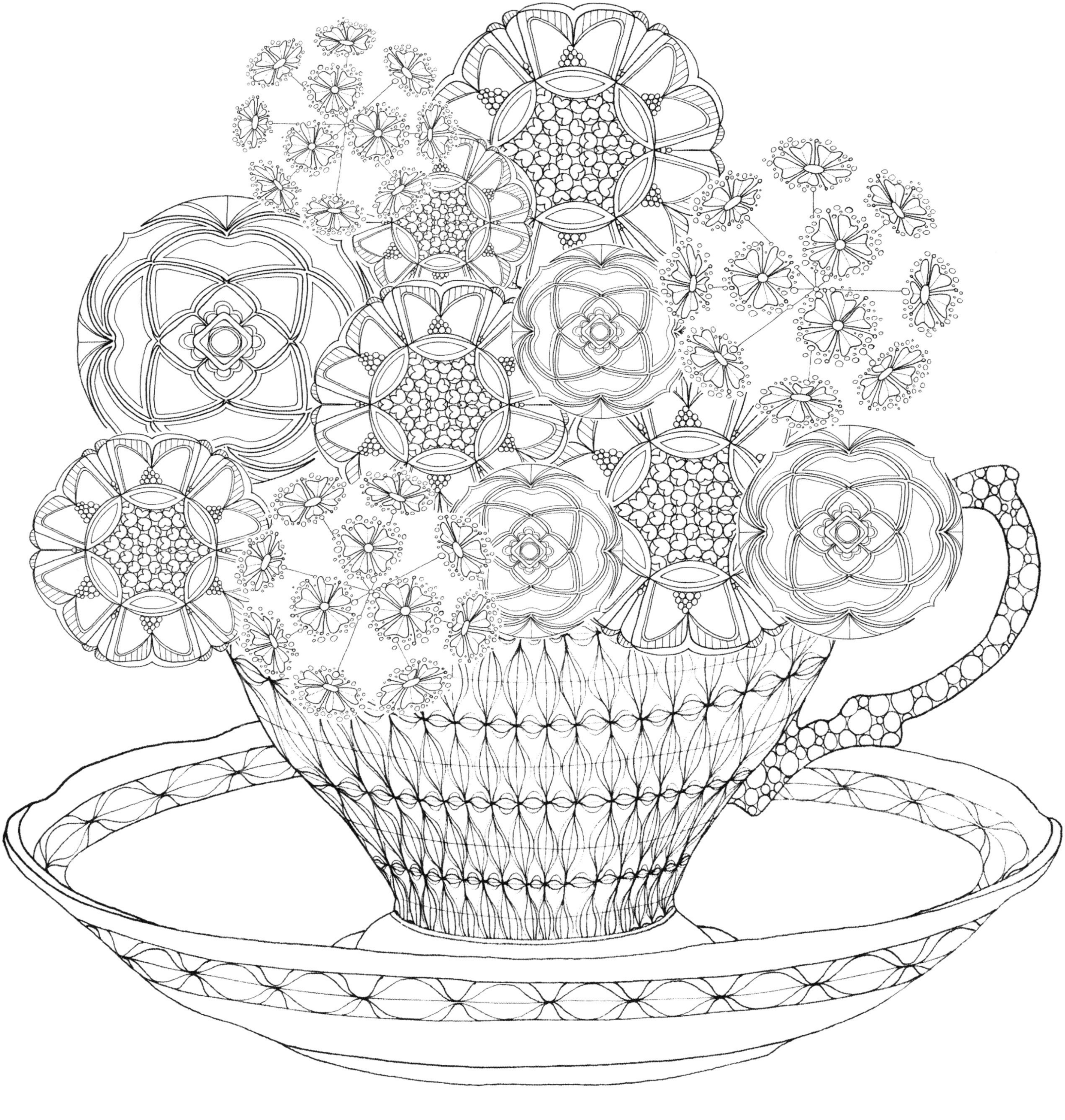

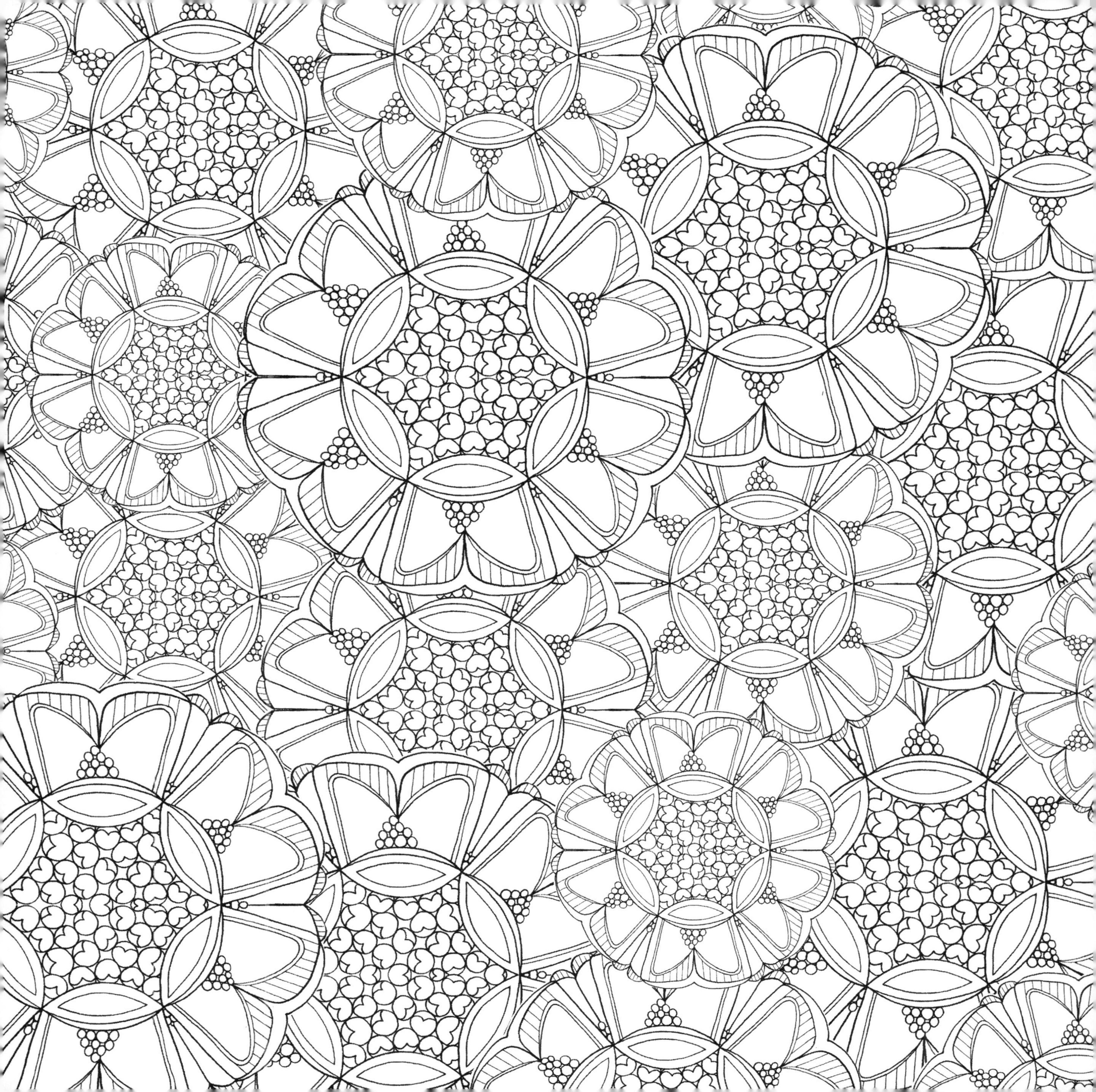

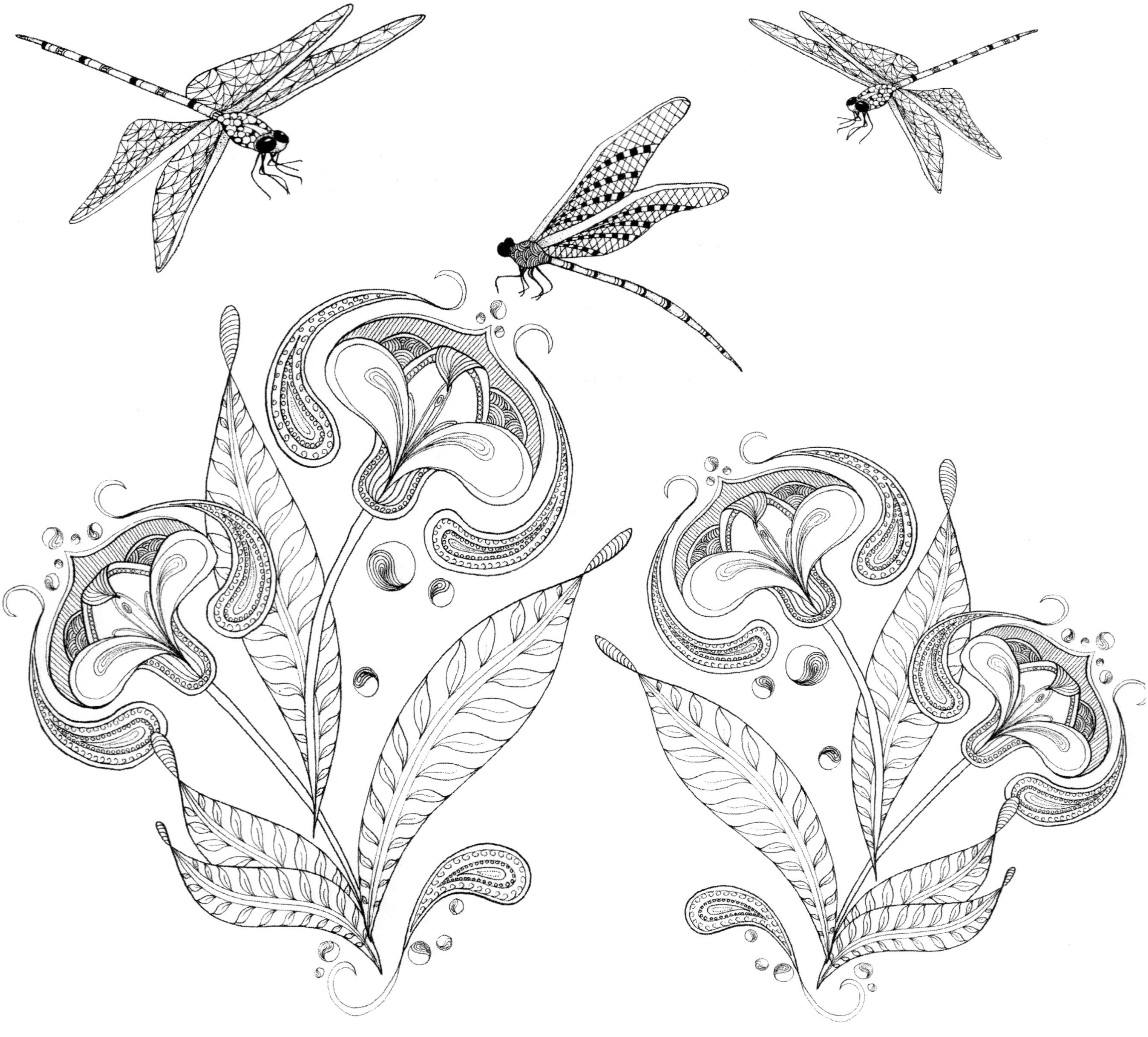

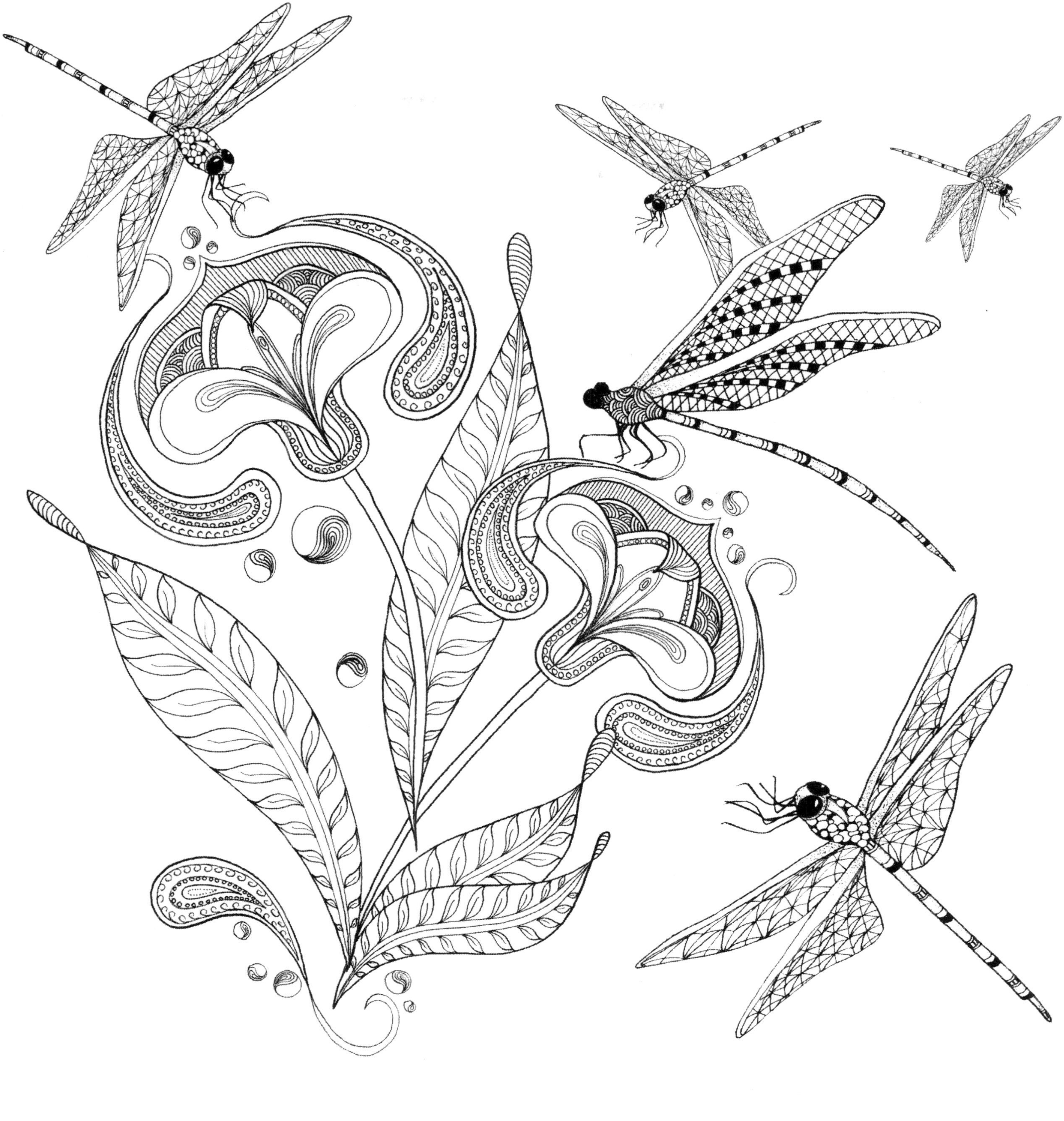

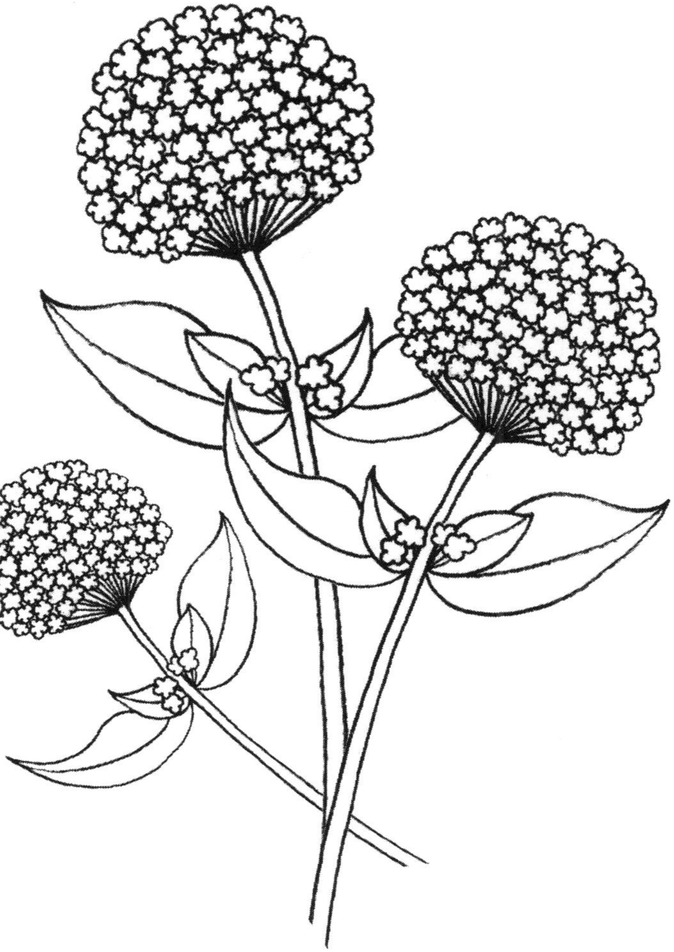

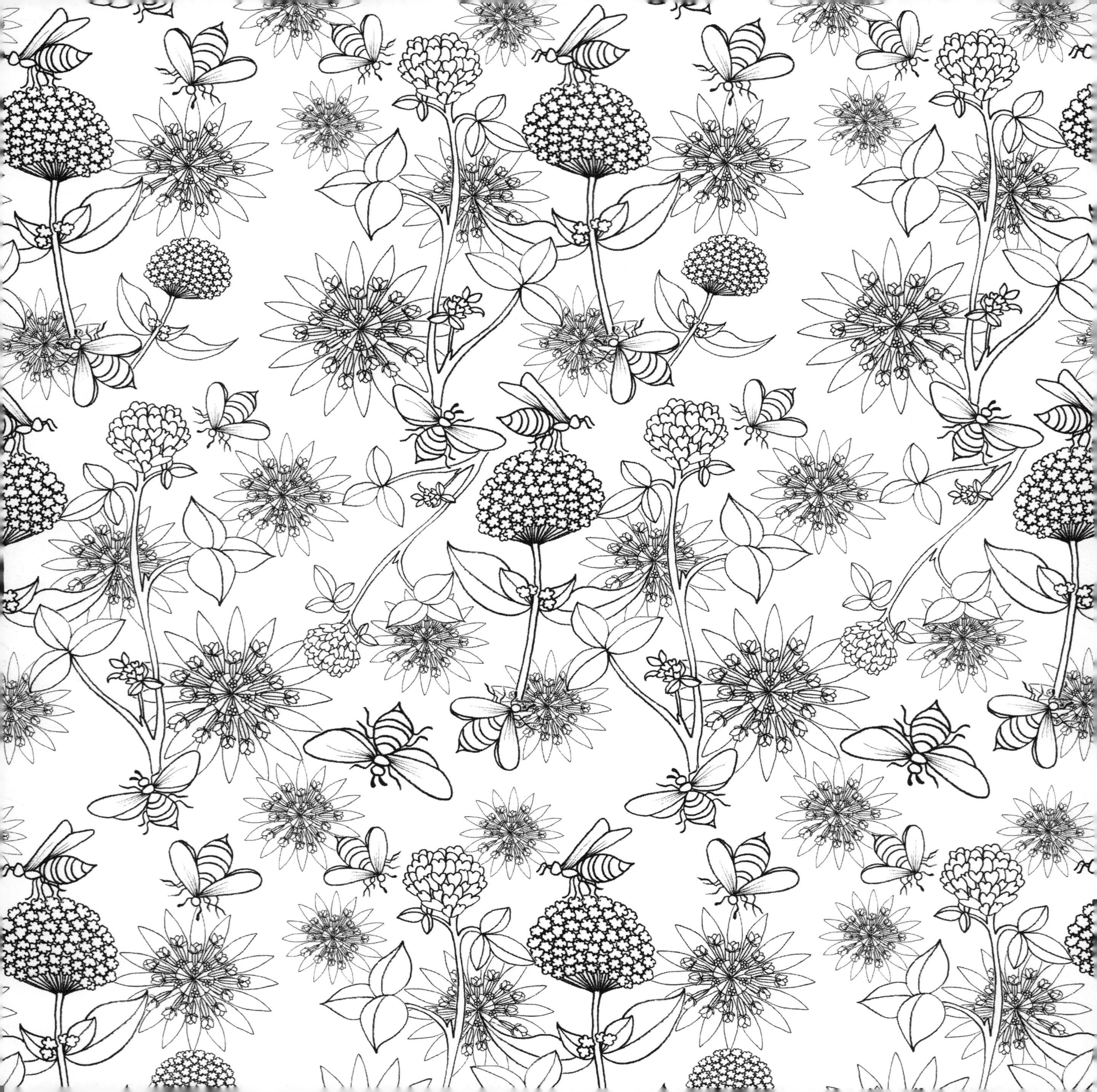

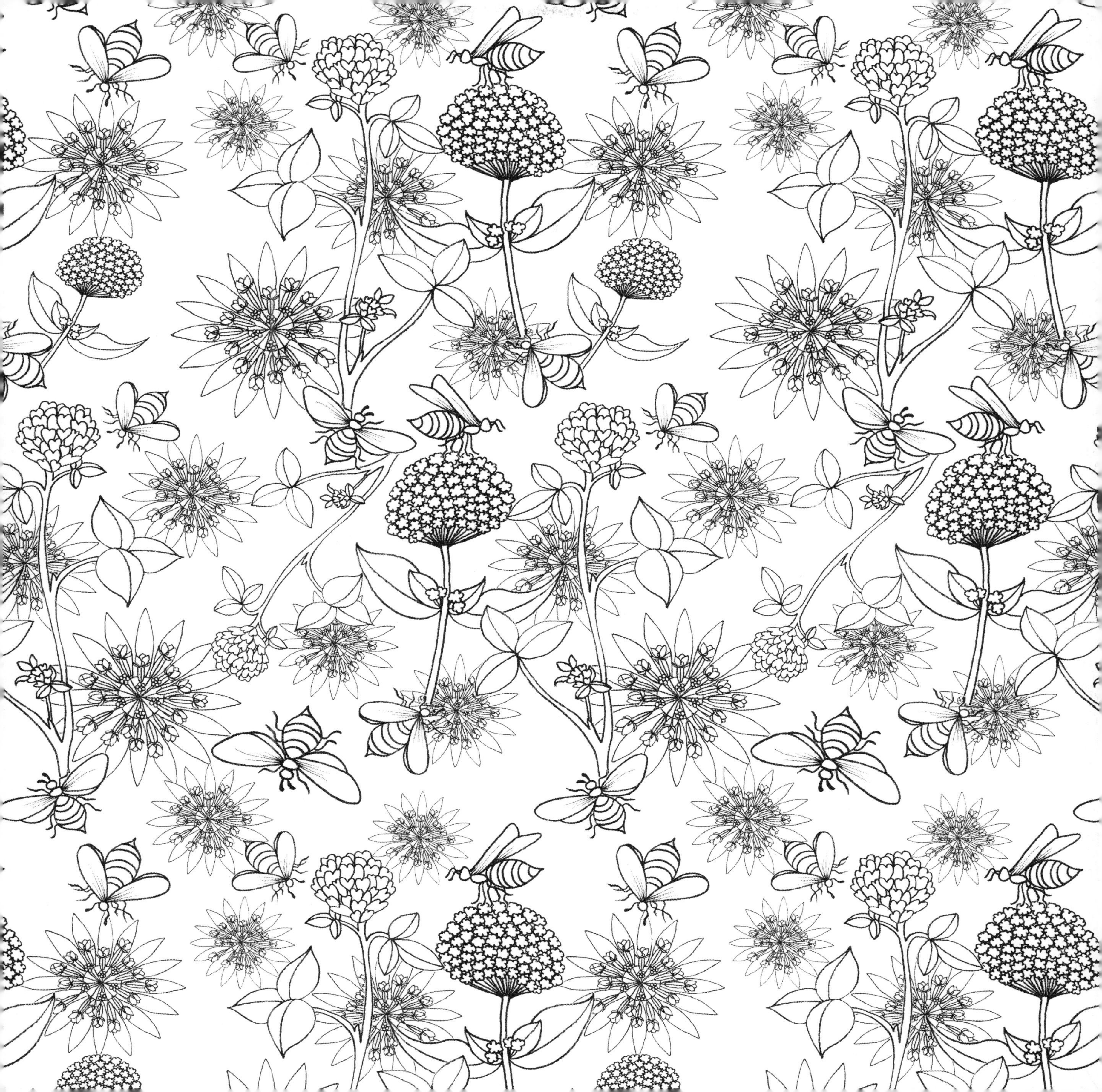

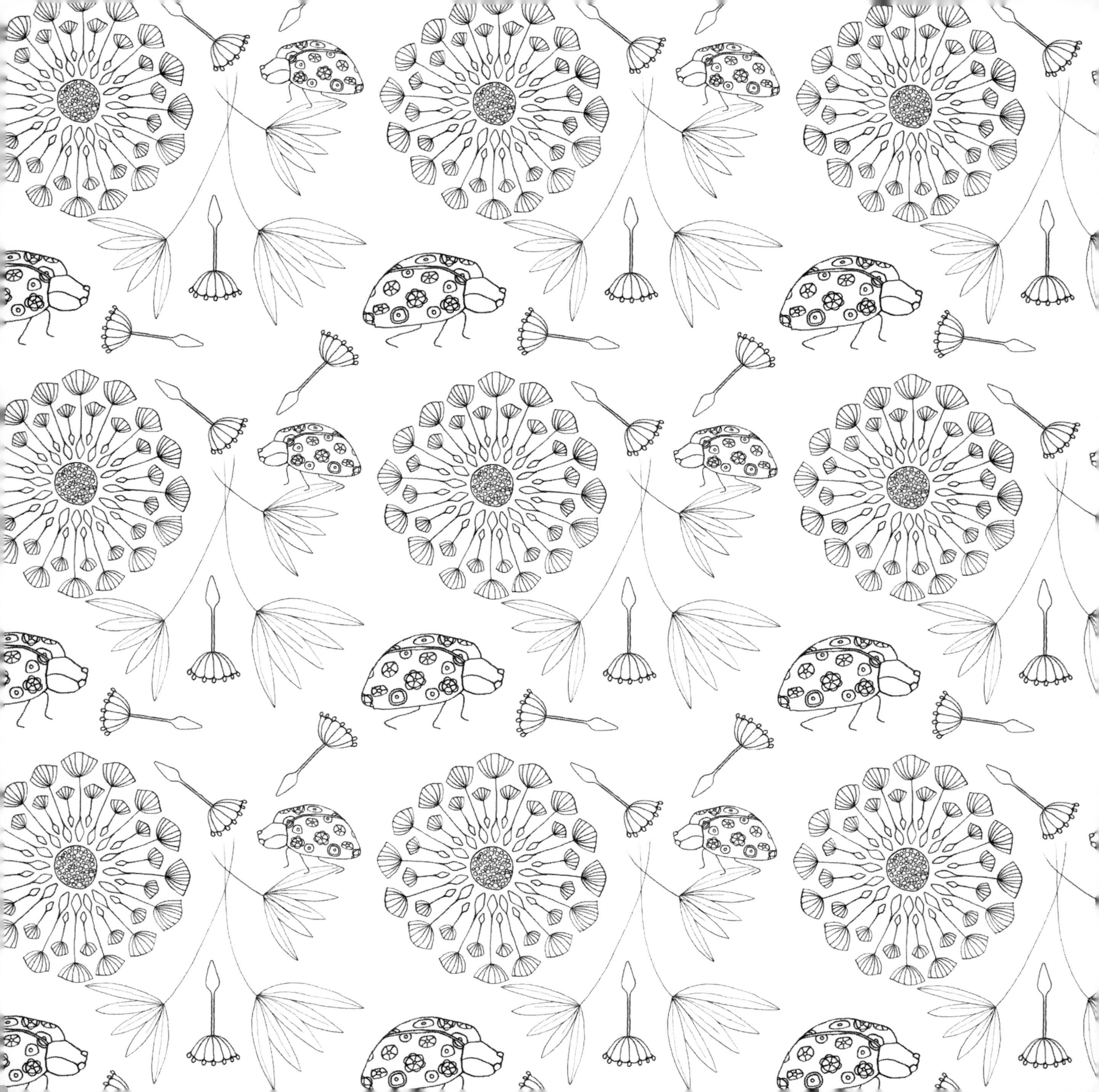

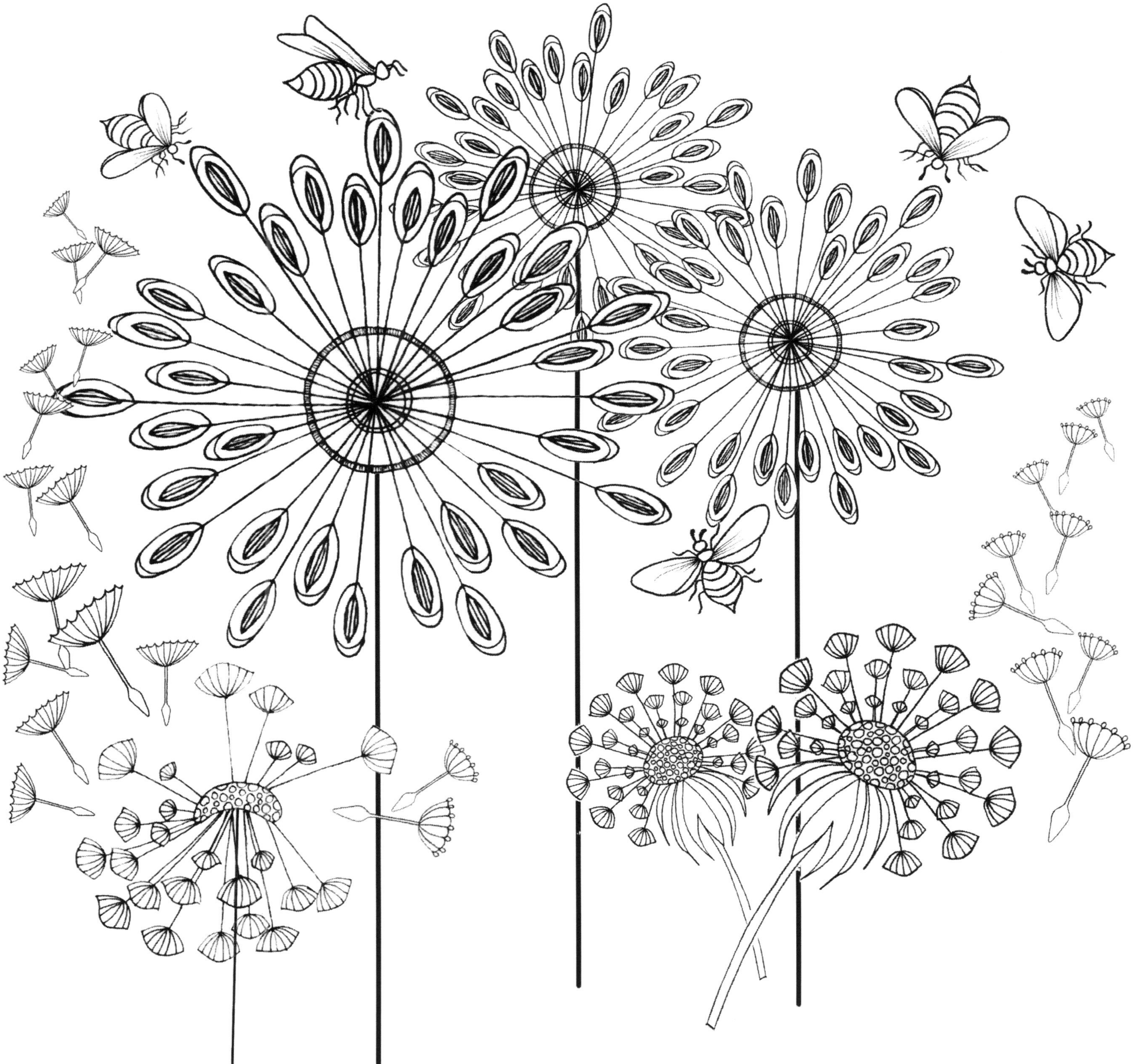

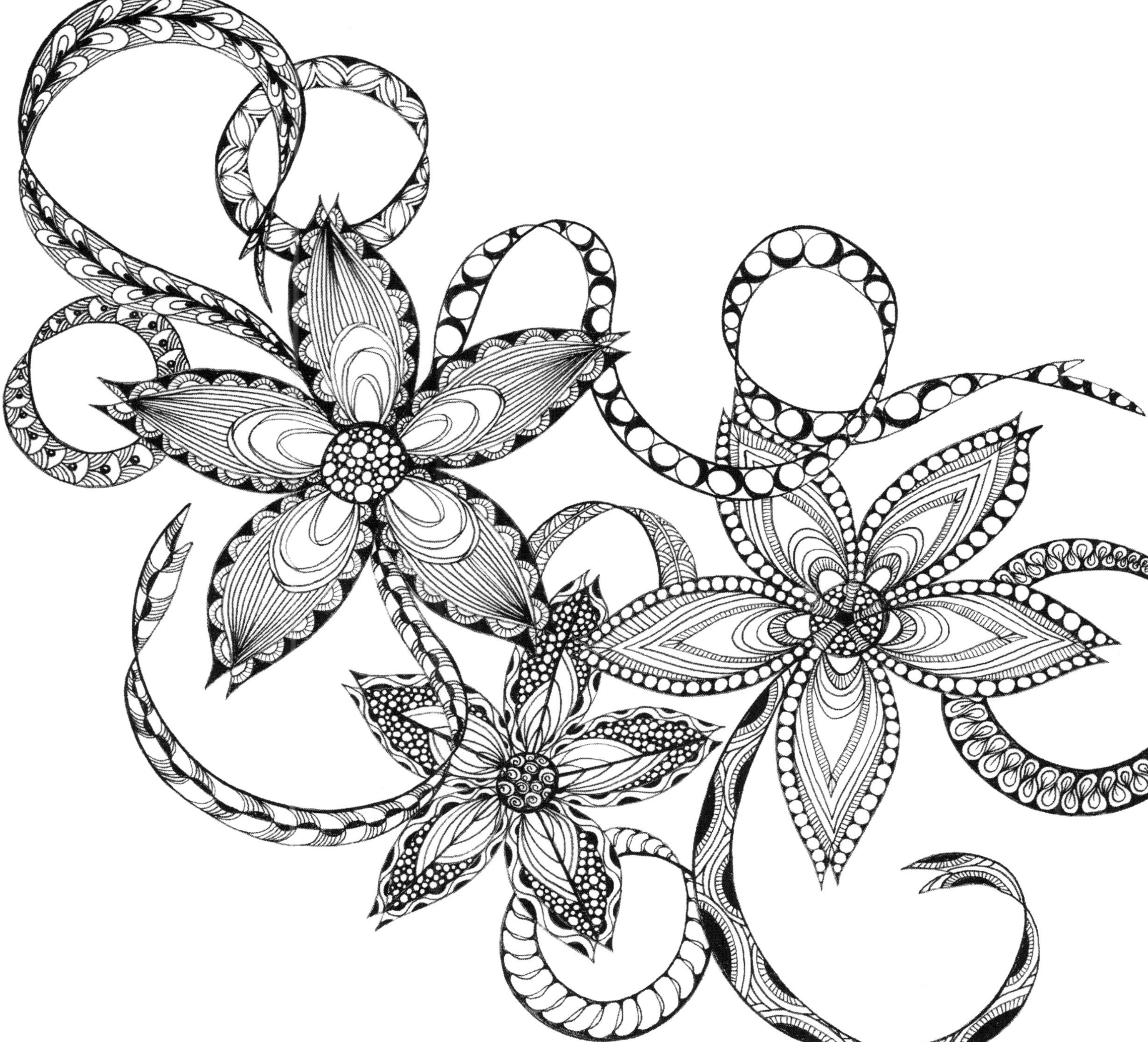

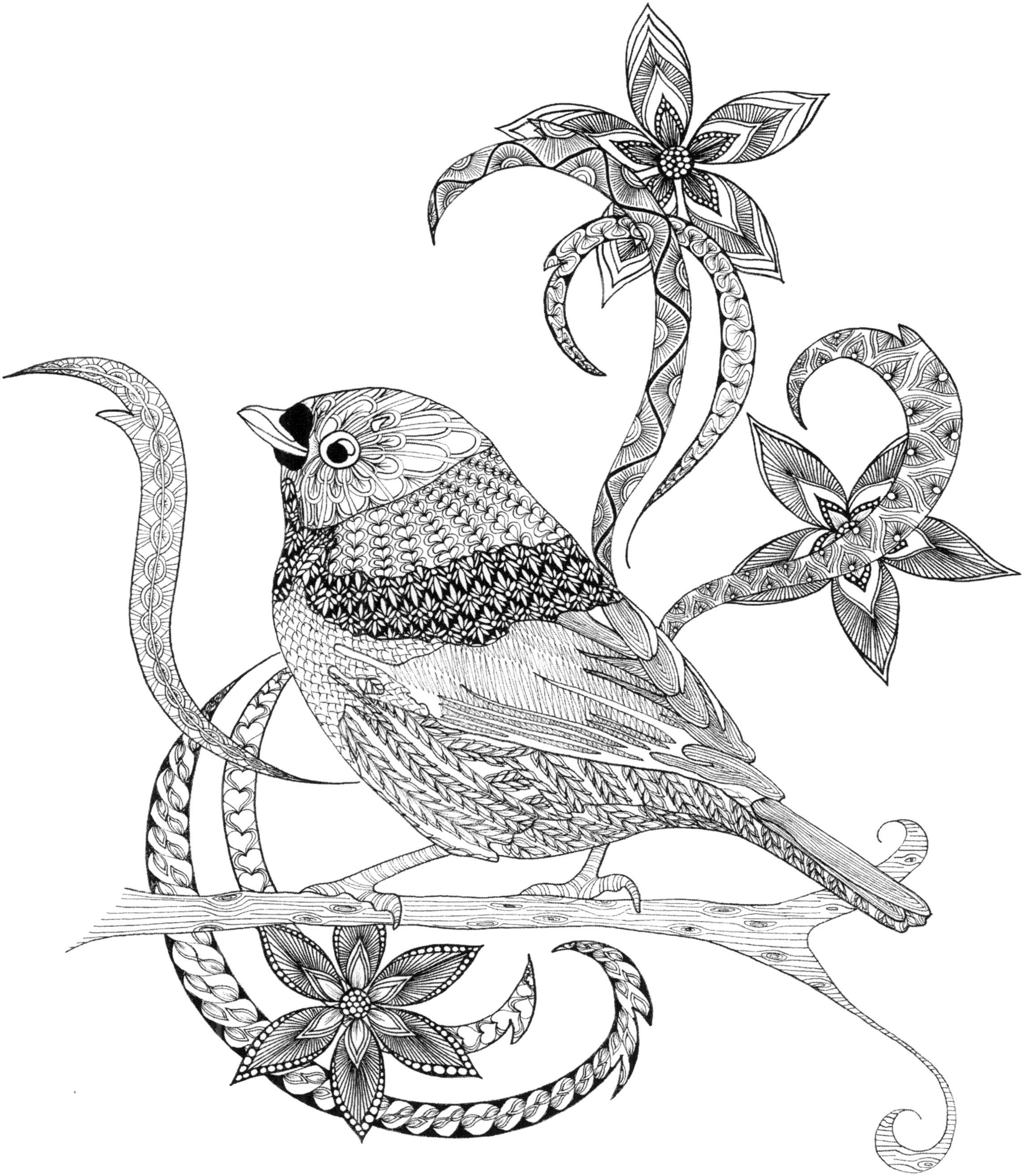

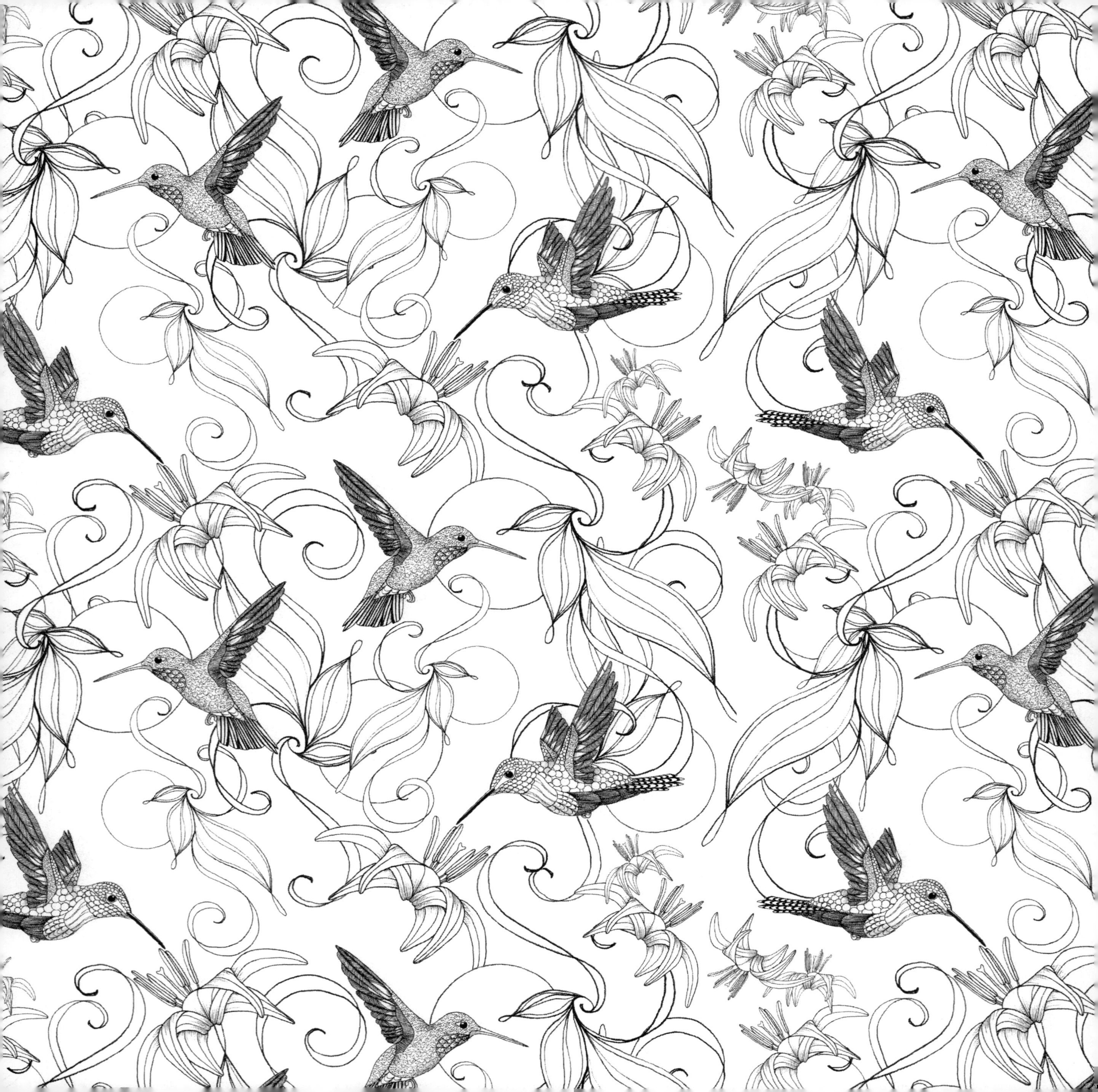

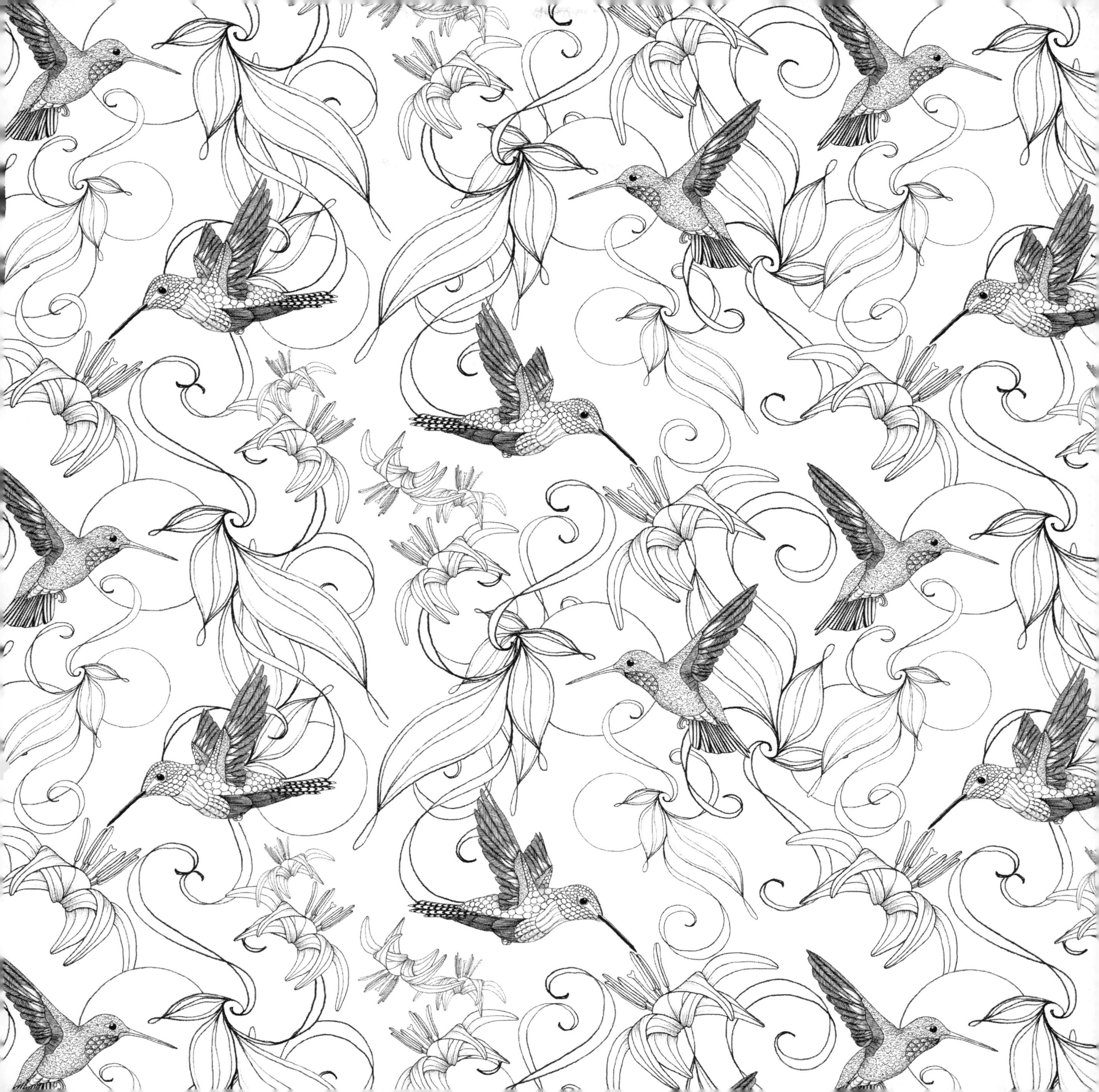

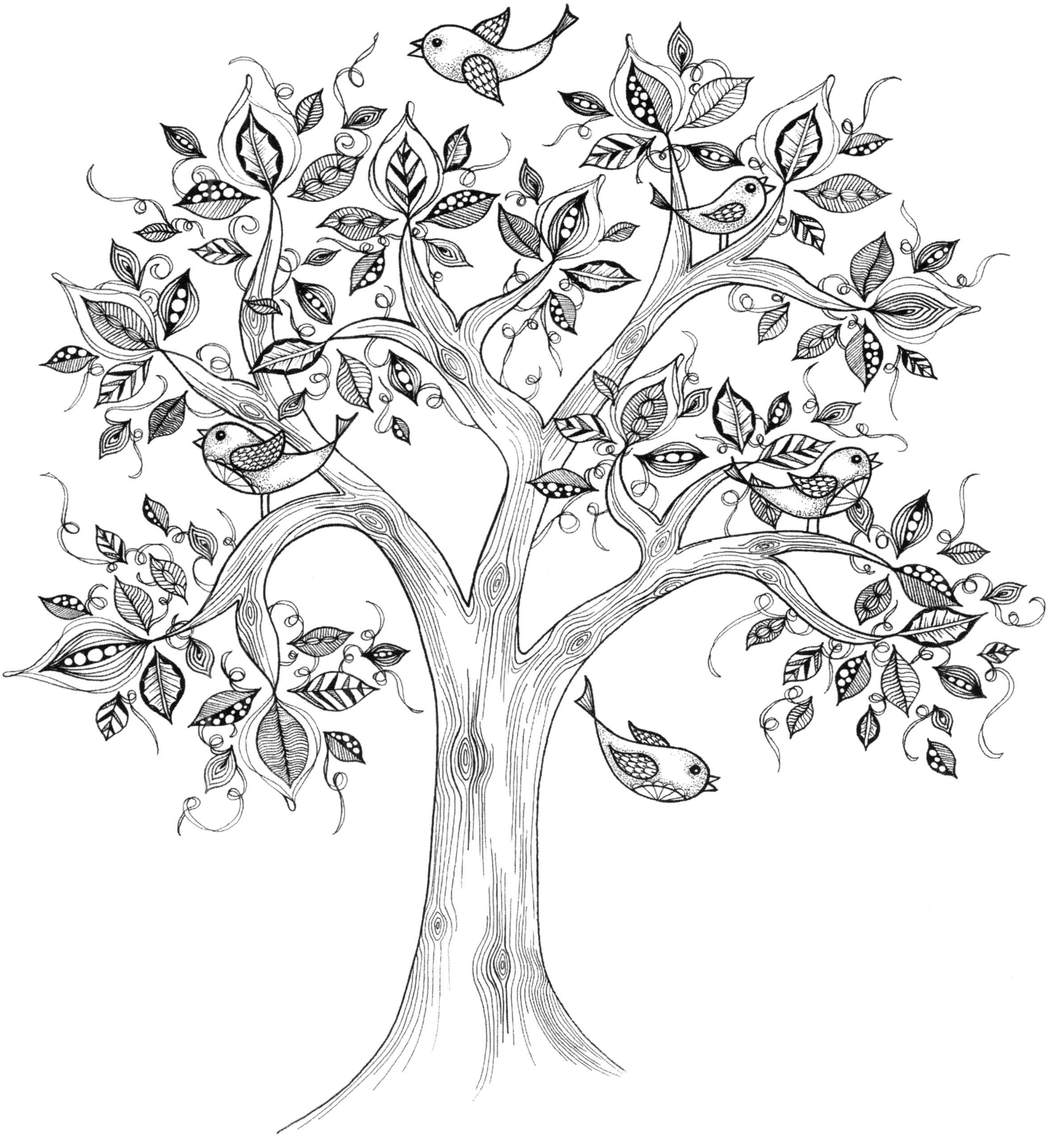

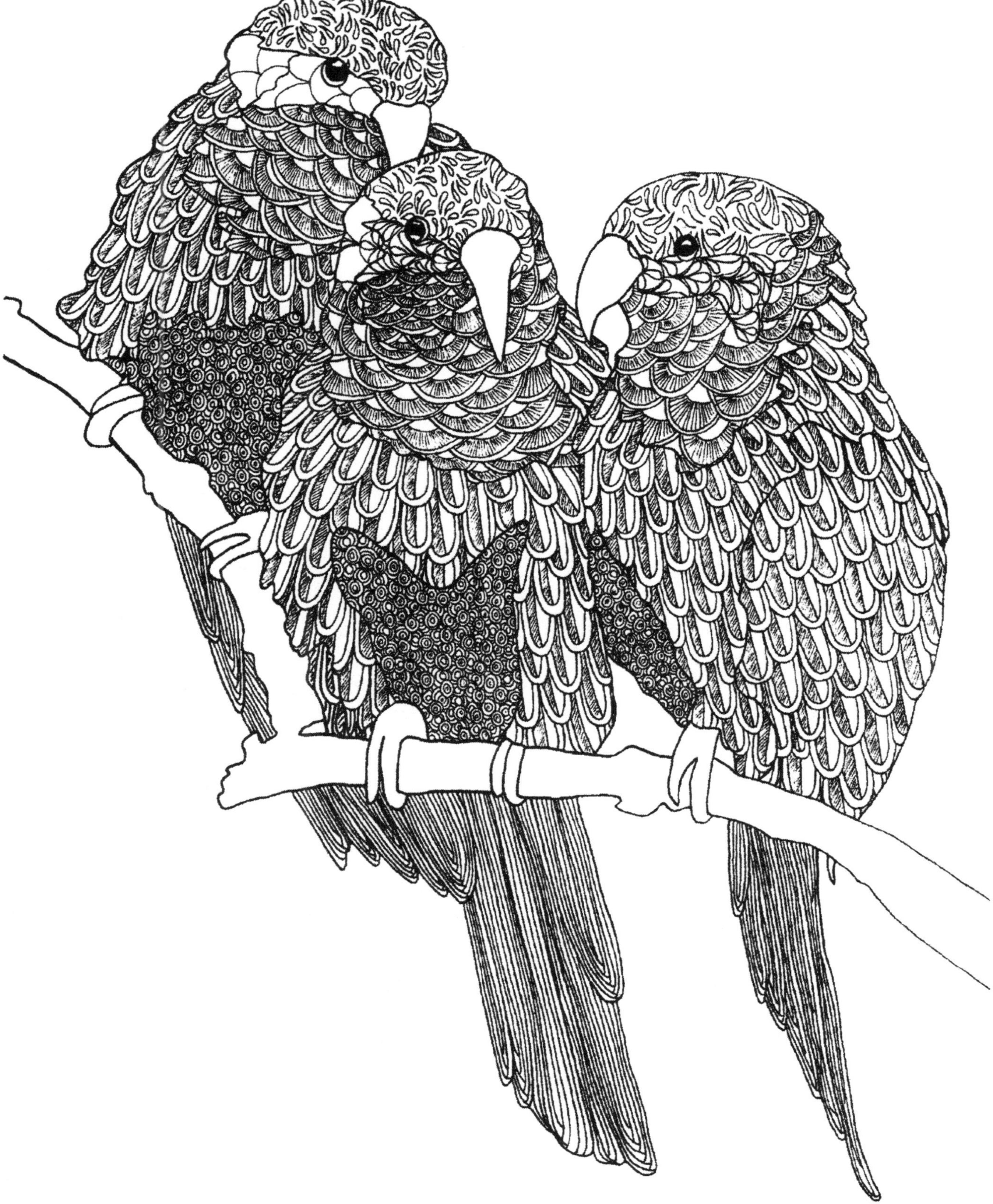

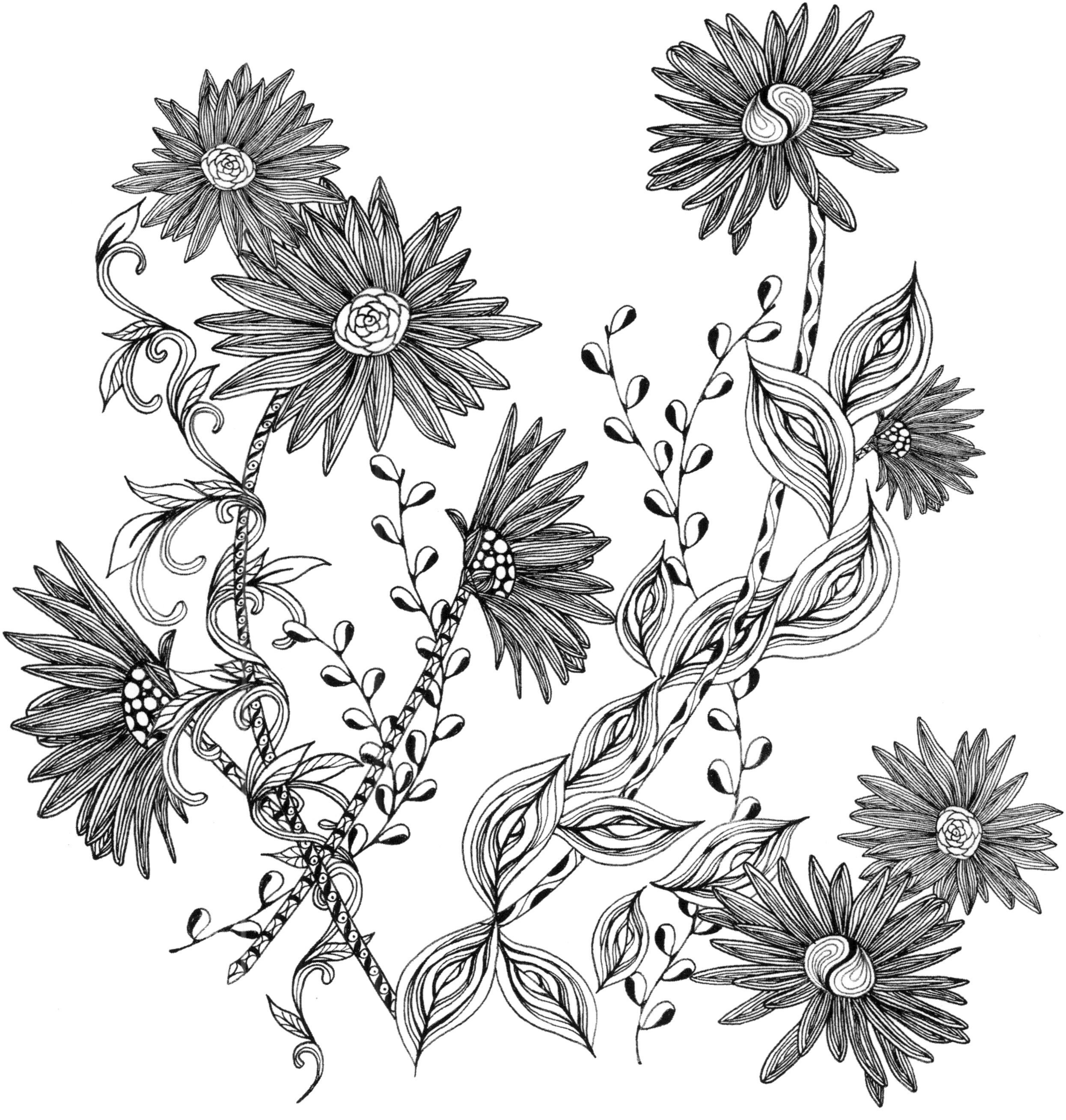

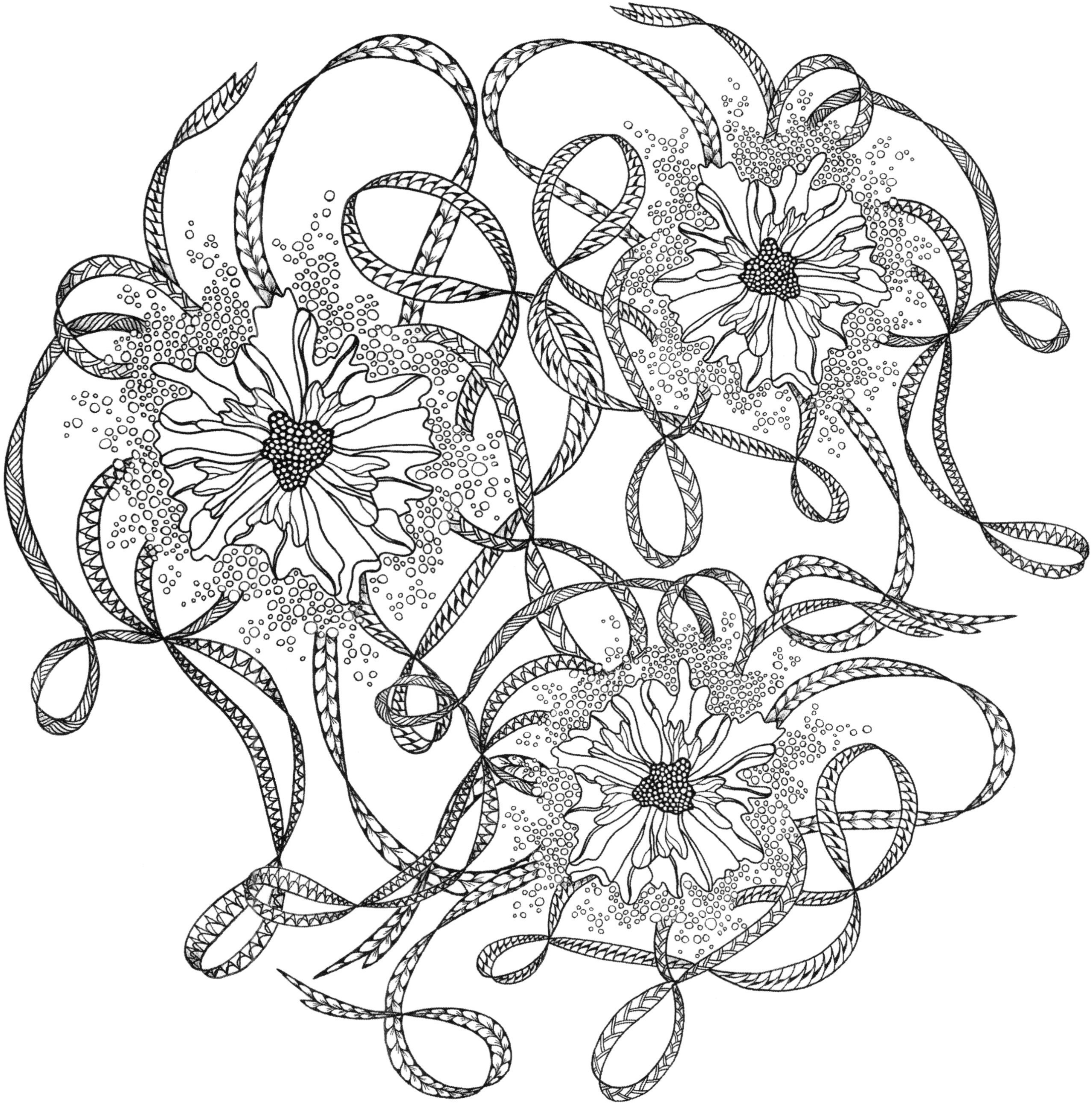

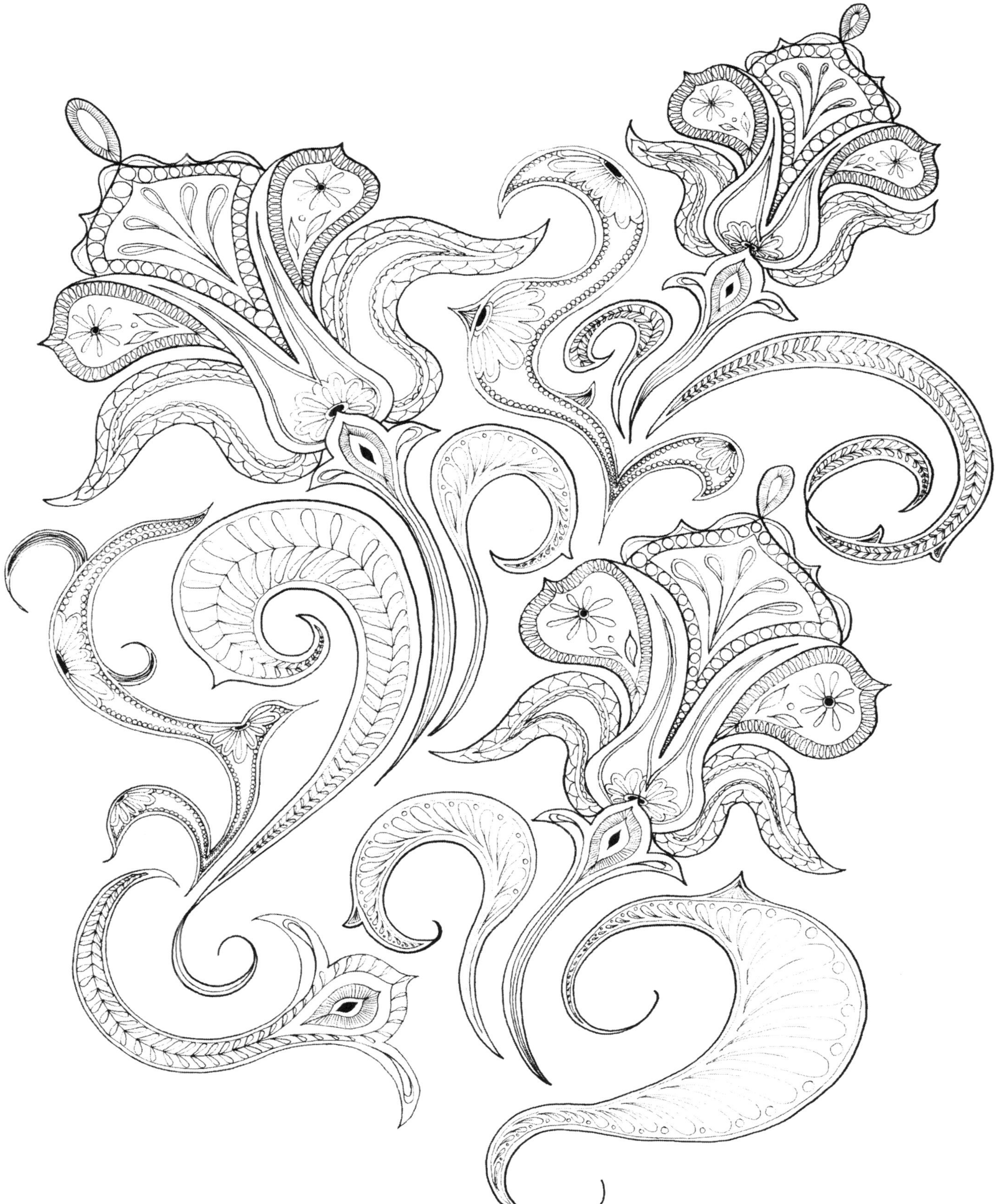

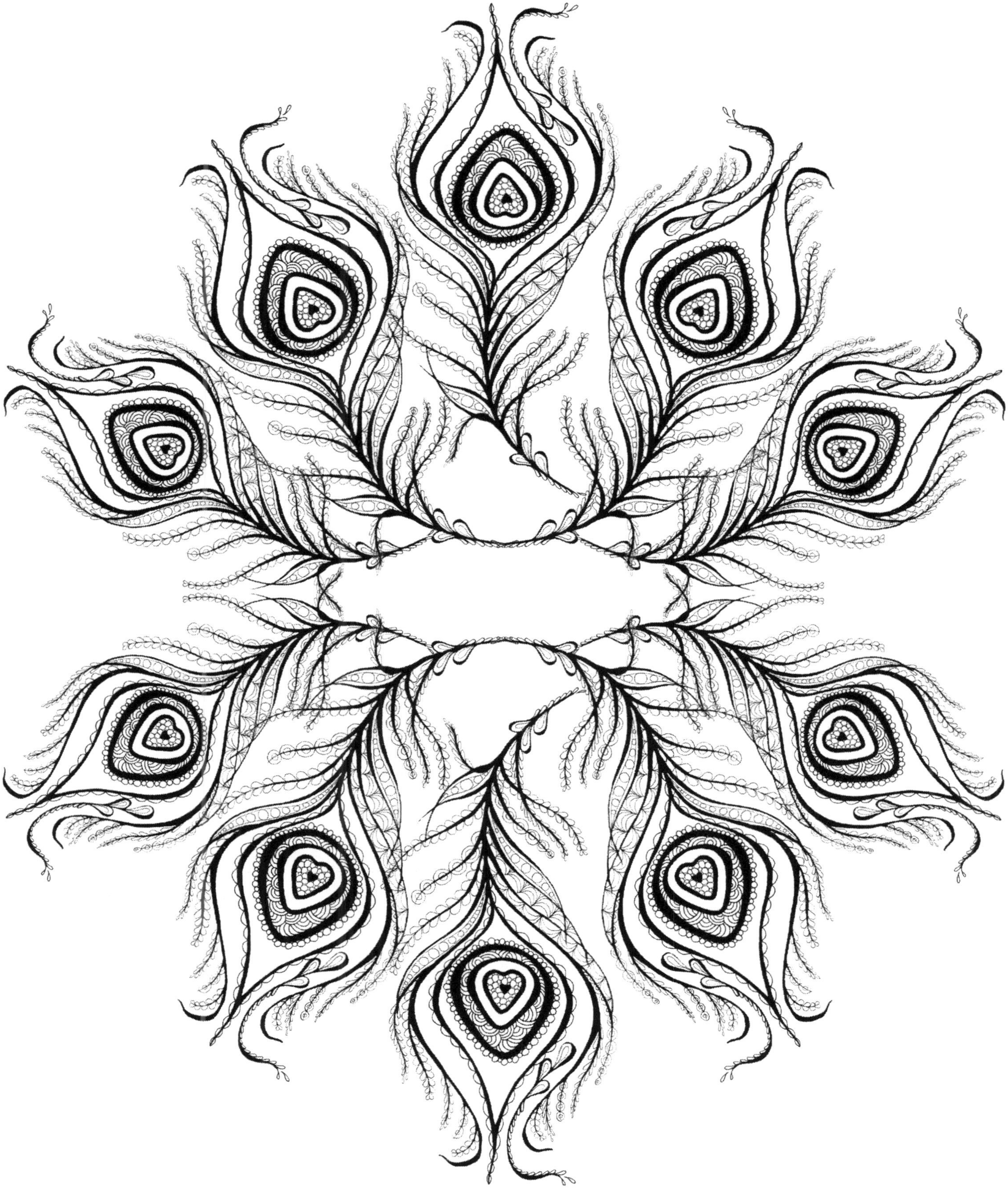

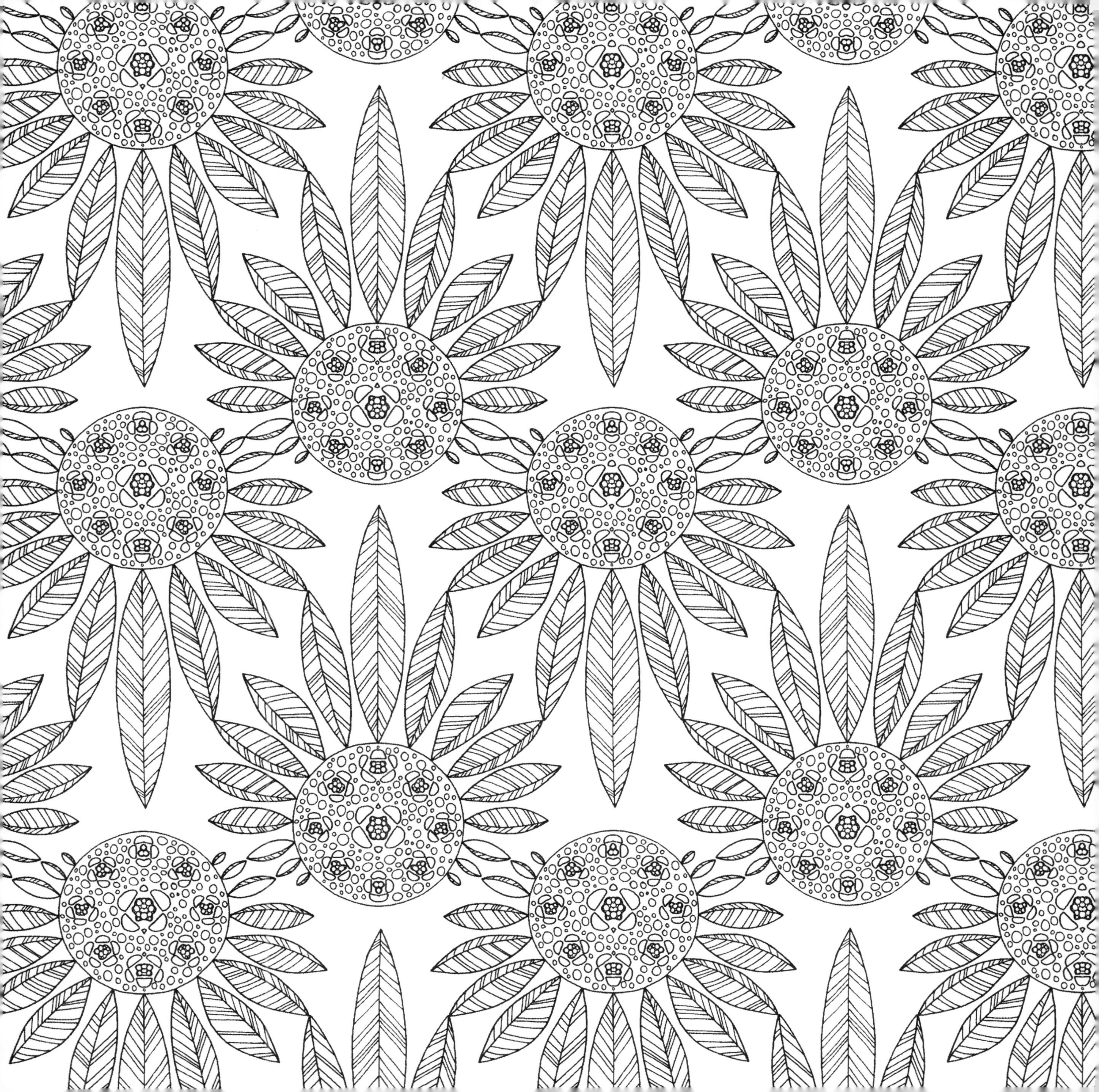

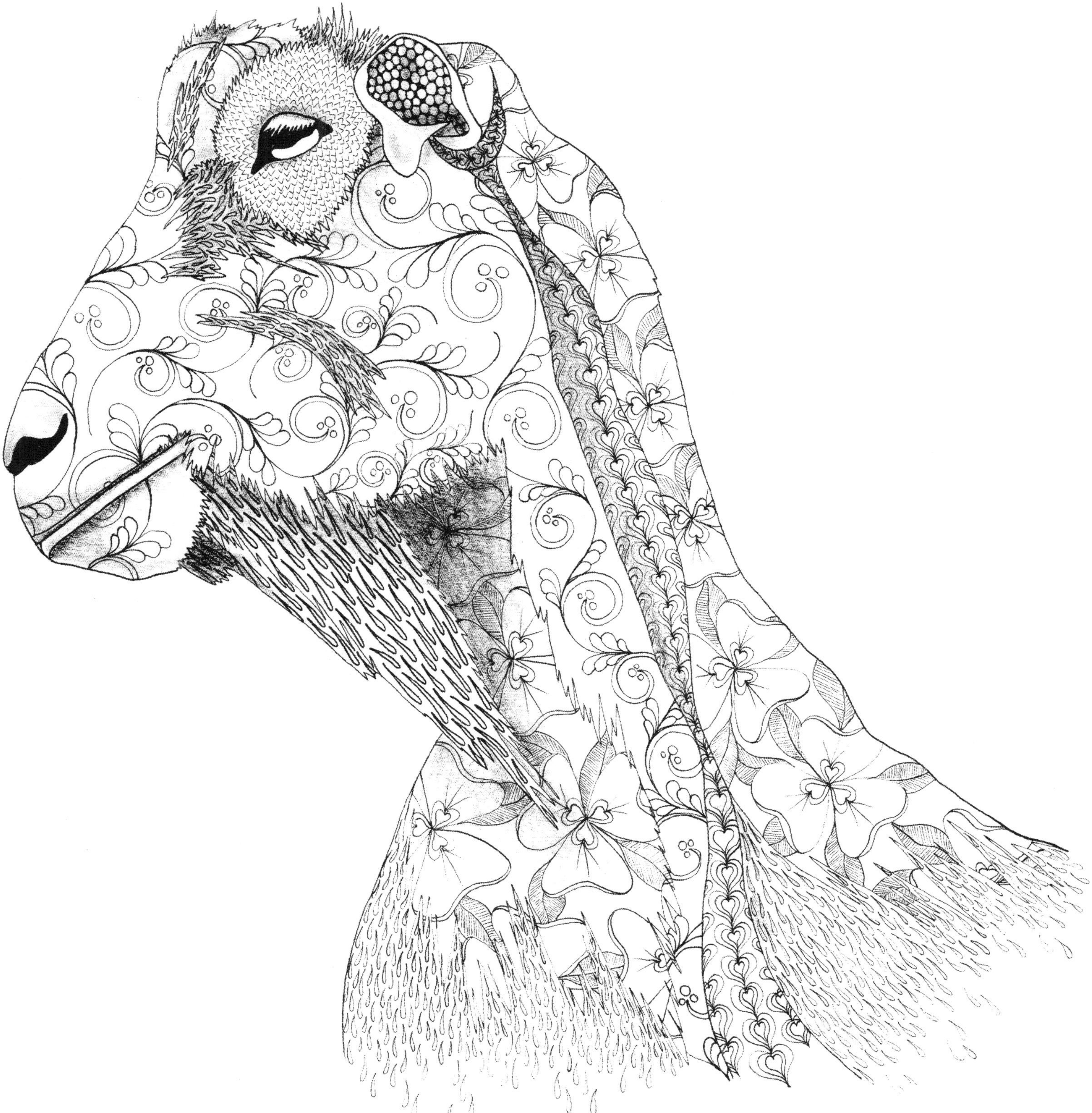